Enjoying

Space

through the

Hubble Lens

Photographs collected from NASA

by Catherine McGrew Jaime

Arp 273 Two Interacting Galaxies

In the constellation Andromeda

Bubble Nebula (NGC* 7635)

In the constellation Cassiopeia

Discovered in 1787 by William Herschel

New General Catalogue of Nebulae and Clusters of Stars

Carina Nebula

In the constellation Carina

Discovered in 1752 by Nicolas-Louis de Lacaille

Cassiopeia A

A Supernova Remnant

In the constellation Cassiopeia

Discovered in 1948 by Martin Ryle

and Francis Graham-Smith

Horsehead Nebula

In the constellation Orion

Recorded in 1888 by Williamina Fleming

IC 342 (Caldwell 5)

A Spiral Galaxy

in the constellation Camelopardalis

Discovered by William Frederick Denning in 1892

M1* Crab Nebula

A Supernova Remnant in the constellation Taurus

Identified in 1731 by John Bevis

*Messier Catalogue of "Messier Objects"

M8 (NGC 6523) Lagoon Nebula

In the constellation Sagittarius

Discovered by Giovanni Hodierna before 1654

M16 (NGC 6611) Pillars of Creation

The Eagle Nebula in the constellation Serpens

Discovered by Jean-Philippe de Cheseaux in 1745

M31 (NGC 224)The Andromeda Galaxy

A Spiral Galaxy in the constellation Andromeda

First described by Abd al-Rahman al-Sufi in 964

M33 (NGC 598)

The Triangulum Galaxy

In the constellation Triangulum

Discovered by Giovanni Battista Hodierna by 1654

M42 (NGC 1976) Orion Nebula

In the constellation Orion

First discovered by

Nicolas-Claude Fabri de Peiresc in 1610

M51a (NGC 5194) Whirlpool Galaxy

Spiral Galaxy in the constellation Canes Venatici

First discovered by Charles Messier in 1773

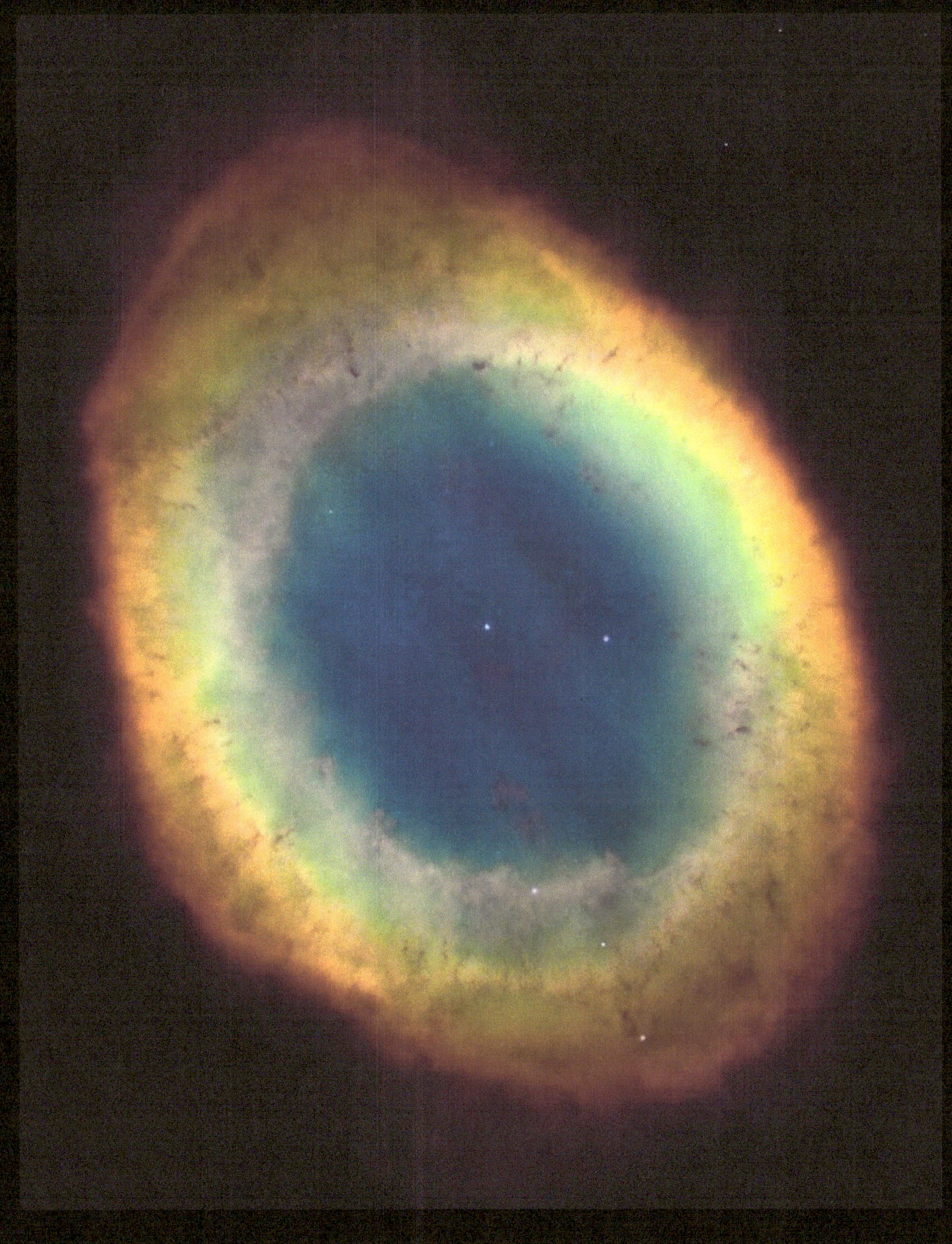

M57 (NGC 6720) Ring Nebula

In the constellation Lyra

First discovered by Charles Messier in 1779

M64 (NGC 4826) Black Eye Galaxy

A spiral galaxy in the constellation Coma Berenices. Discovered by Edward Pigott and Johann Elert Bode in 1779

M82 (NGC 3034) Cigar Galaxy

A starburst galaxy

in the constellation Ursa Major

Discovered by Johann Elert Bode in 1774

M83 (NGC 5236)

The Southern Pinwheel Galaxy

A barred spiral galaxy in the constellation Hydra

Discovered in 1752 by Nicolas Louis de Lacaille

M94 (NGC 4736)

A Spiral Galaxy

in the constellation Canes Venatici

Discovered in 1781 by Pierre Méchain

M96 (NGC 3368)

A Spiral Galaxy in the Constellation Leo

Discovered in 1781 by Pierre Méchain

M100 (NGC 4321)

A Spiral Galaxy

in the Constellation Coma Berenices

Discovered by Pierre Méchain in 1781

M101 (NGC 5457) The Pinwheel Galaxy

A Spiral Galaxy in the Constellation Ursa Major

Discovered in 1781 by Pierre Méchain

M104 (NGC 4594)

The Sombrero Galaxy

A Lenticular Galaxy in the constellation Virgo

M106 (NGC 4258)

A Spiral Galaxy

in the constellation Canes Venatici

Discovered by Pierre Méchain in 1781

NGC 300

A Spiral Galaxy in the constellation Sculptor

NGC 1365

The Great Barred Spiral Galaxy

A Double-Barred Spiral Galaxy

In the constellation Formax

NGC 1569

A Dwarf Galaxy

in the constellation Camelopardalis

NGC 2074

An Emission Nebula in the Tarantula Nebula

NGC 2985

A Spiral Galaxy in the constellation Ursa Major

NGC 4013

A Barred Spiral Galaxy

in the constellation Ursa Major

NGC 4038 & 4039

The Antennae Galaxies

in the constellations Corvus and Crater

NGC 7773

A Barred Spiral Galaxy

in the constellation Pegasus

Orion Nebula

A Diffuse Nebula in constellation Orion

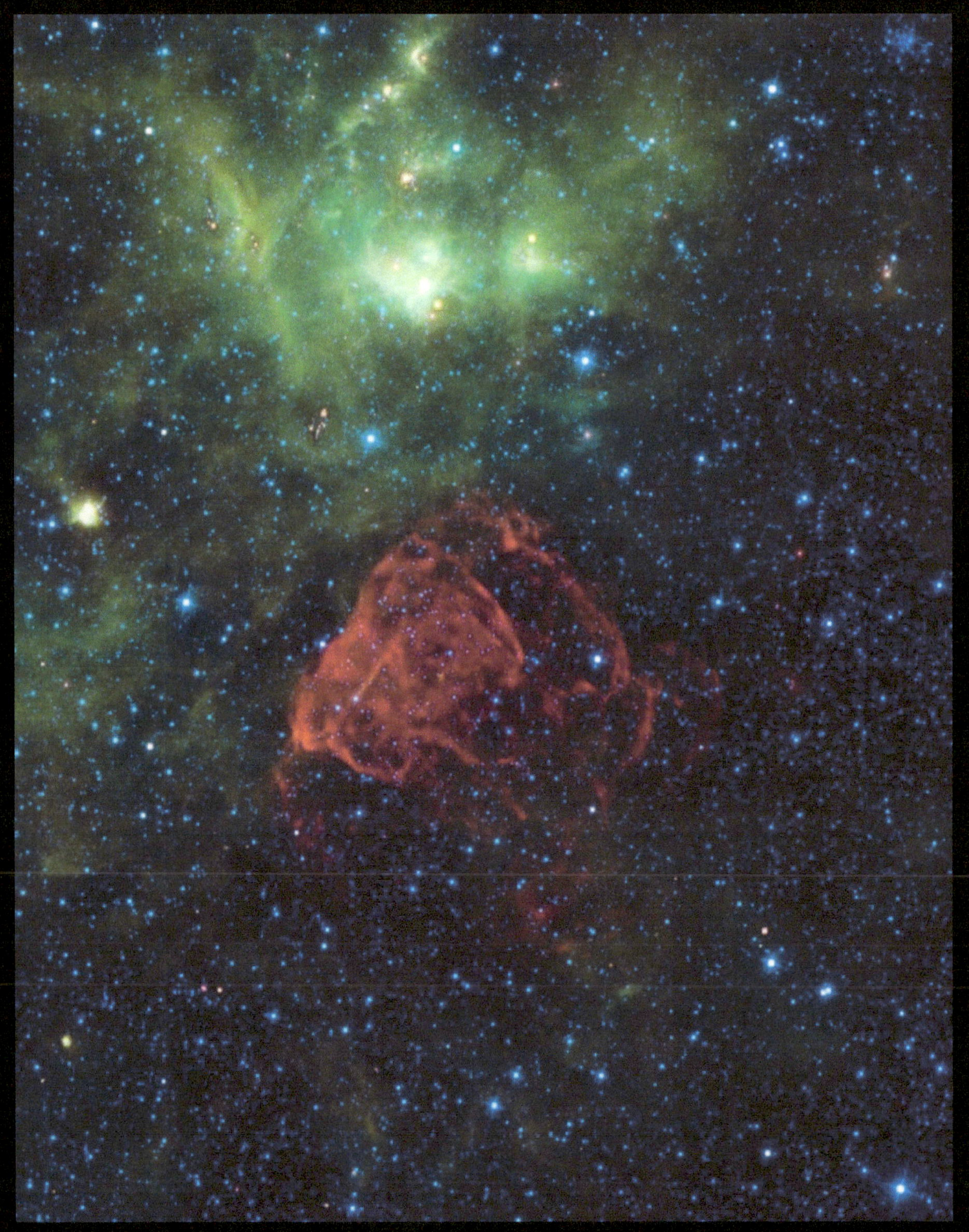

Puppis A

A Supernova Remnant

Sharpless 2-106

An Emission Nebula in the constellation Cygnus

Supernova 1987A

A Supernova in the Large Magellanic Cloud

Supernova Remnant W49B

A Nebula in Westerhout 49

Orion's Sword

A Compact Asterism in the constellation Orion

Veil Nebula

A Supernova Remnant in the constellation Cygnus

www.ingramcontent.com/pod-product-compliance
Lightning Source LLC
Chambersburg PA
CBHW040200240726
48664CB00002B/773